Extraordinary Automobiles

Extrao

Auton

PETER VANN

dinary
obiles

ERALD ASARIA

Motorbooks International
Publishers & Wholesalers Inc.
Osceola, Wisconsin 54020, USA ®

Contents

Published by
Motorbooks International
Publishers & Wholesalers, Inc.
729 Prospect Avenue
Osceola, Wisconsin 54020 USA
©Copyright 1985 by
Motorbooks International

ISBN 0-87938-201-5

Foreword

This book is not just another automotive picture book presenting a collection of traditional shots of that most hackneyed subject — four-wheel motor vehicle productions. Rather, it is an appeal to the senses, a summoning of the great dream, addressed to our longing for escape and our yearning for the exceptional. Peter Vann, one of our best contemporary photographers, has travelled the world to capture the architectural and graphical reality of the machines which, due to the spirit of individuality they embody, have already marked this last quarter century. Peter Vann focuses on people who, in spite of their involvement with an automotive industry which has been shaken continually by unforeseen catastrophes since the early 1970s, successfully resisted the dilution of their mechanical wonders.

Thanks to these people, at a time when the major manufacturers were contending with the new catchwords of drabness (ie. pollution control, fuel consumption, efficiency, safety) and the ideals of creativity and originality were being relegated to the back burner along with other pious hopes, dreams somehow became more dreamlike and the uncommon more exciting. These free-lance designers continued to work in shops and laboratories tucked far away from the madding crowd of productivity to preserve the dream. Men with names like Buchmann, Sbarro, Clenet, Artz, Giugiaro and others, sometimes misconstrued by the public, just kept on "keepin' on" and building their machines. Their names indeed will not be found in gold lettering above the world's great avenues. And Peter Vann literally had to haunt their hideouts in order to immortalize their sometimes secret achievements. Some of their works have already perished down some lost African sand trail or in the steep hairpins of some mechanically grueling rally. Others perhaps are resting in peace in a far-off American private museum. Vann's images are both pure and sophisticated, catching the unaltered creativeness of these lovers of beauty and paying hommage to all of those who carried on the dream even as the automotive giants themselves succumbed to an economic, political and social environment condusive to anything but romanticism.

True, there is ample evidence in defense of the majors. They have gone through the worst of all times since 1970, as the powers that be systematically confronted passion with reason and fancy with stringency. The Majors' car fell in line, became ever more standardized.

These were hard times indeed and even the most prosperous giants faced difficulties that brought them to the brink of bakruptcy. The fourth, ranked giant, AMC, in fact was unable to stay afloat, and the Europeans themselves were soon compelled to merge in the name of profitability. Renault joined up with Volvo and went on flirting with Peugeot, who bought out Citroën. British Leyland met with enormous difficulties. Chrysler began to crumble; Alpha-Romeo called in the Japanese. All the majors faced one storm after another, the first of which was paradoxically called "safety." Carmakers, especially in the USA, were required to entirely reconsider their designs to meet a whole slew of stringent new requirements from "crash testing" to roadholding (the latter being in fact well-deserved in some cases). At the same time, the second generation of Naderites launched new harassment tactics and the government followed suit. The ecologists too joined in, similarly believing that engines kill, albeit differently : they pollute. This meant revising the power trains, controlling emissions with ever more complex exhausts. Such attacks on the automobile were by no means limited to Detroit. US Porsche, for one, had to face the possibility of no longer offering its great 911 America. The best-loved sports car, with its rear engine, couldn't accommodate an exhaust system long enough to include all the regulation baffles. So, with the 911 under siege, the Stuttgart carmaker was forced to fall back and develop a front-engined generation of 924s, 928s, 944s and such. Just as everything seemed to be getting under control, the worst broadside of all suddenly hit, in 1973 : the oil crisis.

The mad rush for mileage was on and was incidentally tied to two contradictory requirements : safety (more weight and thus less miles to the gallon) and emission control (with systems absorbing power and therefore energy). The computers themselves, in all their glory, were losing their Basic.

Shortly thereafter, in 1974, I was invited to visit the world's largest automotive research facility — the GM Tech Center in Detroit — to be introduced to the latest designs for the 1980s. I was given the exceptional honor of being shown the generation of future machines — machines which I had imagined as sort of syblings of the lunar module or of electric cars from a sci-fi comic. Here I was, after all, in this universe of scientists, engineers, computer experts and stylists with apparently unlimited means at their disposal. My credentials were deemed so good that I was even given a preview of GM's top prototypes — five years before they were to become a reality! — a preview of the Cadillacs-to-be of the eighties... and these Cadillacs had truncated tails like the postwar Rolls. While everything in the science fiction department, in the department of the exceptional, of fantasy, had been relegated to the automotive museum at the Tech Center entrance. There just *were no more* astonishing prototypes, no more dream cars. I even suspected for a while that I was the object of a joke, at which point it was disclosed to me "off the record" and for my ears only that the main focus of all the engineers for the years 1980 to 1990 was a dull Diesel like the ones which had been hauling cab drivers and truckers around Europe for a decade. Alas, when 1980, then 81 and 82 came along, I had to recognize that the GM people had given me the whole truth and nothing but the truth. Inventive genius had effectively been muzzled and the great dream was dead, killed by a mere phrase : "Meet the regulation".

The Design Department, in a room the size of a football field, was hardly more exciting : the stylists now worked to a computer terminal. By punching a few keys, for example, they could introduce a coded suitcase into a trunk which automatically changed dimensions in 3D on the CRT to assume a new shape basically dictated by a sacrosanct set of specifications, stored precisely to adapt to the suitcase. I remember thinking that the final configuration of GM's most beautiful car was probably being decided right on that screen. The computer had taken over from the pencil — a savior for the vacillating marriage between the industry, creativity and government regulations. Everything, from the height of the tail lights, to the drag coefficient and the size of occupant protections was designed to "meet the regulations." The car haters were moving in for the kill, taking advantage of the recession to proclaim themselves as the high priests of the dull car and to challenge speed itself, as well as creativeness and everything else that was still car and dream. The uncommon car seemed doomed.

In February 1974, in the wake of the Yom Kippur War, the oil supply to Europe was temporarily threatened. Certain governments, such as those of France and Italy, hypocritically seized this opportunity to impose aberrant speed limits. I was in the area of Maranello at the time, visiting the Ferrari production plants, as well as the Maserati, Lamborghini and Bertone plants down the road. Some of them were on the verge of bankruptcy. The companies had had to rent open fields surrounding their workshops to store their finest products, some of which were already sinking into muddy soil. Speed, luxury and refinement were no longer salable and no one would have wagered on their future in that dark hour.

And even still, there was life left in the old dream. Sure, Ghia was now part of Ford, but its little emblem would henceforth provide the manufacturer that touch of fantasy it had lacked. The Granada, as well as World Cars like the Escort, would soon put it to good use treating themselves to that vital note of individuality opening the way to the luxury car market. Fiat too had begun to rely to a greater extent on Ferrari to glamourize its sedans. While Audi and Renault had moved decisively into racing to gain world recognition for a product which the 1980s required to be as personalized, even as prestigious as possible.

A new watershed had been reached and spectacular changes were at hand, one of the most noticeable examples of which concerned the convertible top, considered moribund in the seventies in light of the "safety first" attitude that reigned and the "must" of air conditioning. But when the last of the Cadillac Eldorado convertibles were auctioned off in Las Vegas, they drew record bids. Around 1978, when it was learned that the convertible Beetle was on the verge of becoming an extinct specie, the last models were fought over tooth and nail. And in 1980, VW's new Golf/Rabbit Cabriolet was wildly acclaimed. Introduced as a marginal product, it soon became the symbol of escape, *joie de vivre,* and sophistication. The German body builder, Karmann, was soon sollicited by Ford Europe, sorry to have been caught without a convertible Escort. Well, Ford had to wait until 1984 to see its XR3 convertibles produced on assembly lines that can't even meet the demand. Just as Talbot regretfully realized in 1982 that Pininfarina's output of 30 Samba Cabriolets per day would only meet about half of its orders, and in the same year Jaguar announced a convertible XJS for 1983 while Fiat hastily put out a 124 replica of its cabrio-Bertone.

At the next Paris Auto Show, French coachmaker Heuliez, who survived the depression years thanks to his work on buses and trucks, displays a Fuego-based convertible that catches the eye of Renault's Chief Executive. The prototype is without a price tag and trimmed with fine leather. Renault's enthusiam for the dream maker's prototype convertible may on that very day determine his destiny through 1990. Renault, Heuliez, Pininfarina and other even more surprising convertibles are included in this album.

The car haters cried victory too soon. Never before have the artisans of the unique been so sought after. Other examples abound : Citroën's BX, introduced at the same '82 auto show. "Little" Bertone's design has been selected by the Paris giant's design department. In '83, the design for the popular Fiat Uno goes to Giugiaro. VW does not deny that it has been providing dozens of cars to the genius of fine finishing and electronics, Buchmann, to transform inexpensive Polos and Golfs into sophisticated works of art. VW France now officially markets a 16-valve Golf designed by Oettinger, an engine magician, which is almost an outright challenge to the make's marketing rules. Indeed, never before has VW officially recognized even the most talented customizers. This time, the Golf 16 S will be sold by the entire VW network. Buchmann and Oettinger are also in this album, along with the Alpinas, those fantastically performing BMWs wholeheartedly accepted by the Munich automaker.

Commonness and rationalness have begun to retreat before talent and originality. At the 1982 Paris Show, again, the Ford Sierra with its entirely innovative styling was the center of attention. Its designer, Patrick Le Quement, confides that the Sierra owes nothing — at least at the start — to the computer, but is the child of his team's pencils. Dreaming has regained some of its legitimacy.

A similar trend has appeared in the advertising world. Having used the language of economy, of reason, soberness and "ennui", they are returning to a language of emotion and, one might say, of "polysensualism." The new Talbot is Brazilian and dances the Samba. The Citroën BX no longer even makes an appearance in the first posters of the campaign. Instead, it is symbolized by a loving couple in a natural or seaside setting. These "teasers" serve to introduce the first pictures of the BX itself in subsequent ads with a white, block-lettered copy line proclaiming that the BX "lives." Rationality retreats further and the dream is reborn. Those who were looked down upon as mere survivors and hangers-on of bygone days now appear as the new pioneers. This book is dedicated to these survivors and pioneers.

For there were some who held the fort throughout the years of hardship — a handful of craftsmen of the "Resistance" in Britain and the USA who dared to venture from the ever more stringently marked trail, building strange machines known as "replicars", extraordinarily combining modern mechanical genius and nostalgia-ridden body designs. The Replicars introduce the emotional, the superfluous, the baroque and the anti-conventional; they suggest the heyday of the Hispanos, the Auburns, the Bugattis while at the same time partly conforming to the new rules. A select number of these unyielding craftsmen are also represented in the pages that follow.

In the US, and especially in California, where the regulations were the most draconian, the small car-makers made it a point of honor to produce machines defying any measure of reasonableness, whether in the form of crystal-windowed Clenets, 1,200-hp engined Vectors, 6-seater limousine versions of the Ferrari 400 and what not. There, amidst the palmtree-lined straightaways a few blocks from Hollywood and the Pacific, extravagance has been made car.

Peter Vann has devoted an entire chapter to these anti-conformist "weird wheelers," which many readers may consider to be the most beautiful photos of all. They're at the end of the book, laid out pell-mell under "Made in USA."

For any attempt at order in dreamland would be an impossible undertaking. On the whole, however, we have broken the book down into rather subjective categories for the reader's convenience. Thus one chapter is devoted to the perfectionists — those who through minor touchups transform a simple Mini or an already impressive Mercedes into a true artwork. They are British, such as Wood and Pickett, German such as Artz, Belgian such as Duchatelet or Italian geniuses such as Pininfarina, Giugiaro, Bertone — names from which anything can be expected. Even those most up to date on the subject may yet find some surprises in this chapter; admirable profiles which we are no longer astonished at finding in modern art museums alongside the sculptures of leading contemporary artists and the models and drawings for which may be auctioned off at

Sotheby's for example, sometimes at a higher price than the established art around them. Another chapter is devoted to machines built in a spirit of performance. This is the chapter of the magicians — those who've found new horsepower for engines that were often already endowed with considerable power — such as Oettinger and Alpina, Lotus and Lamborghini, and even Lancia and Renault. There are also those who, out of their own madness or that of super-rich customers, conceive machines that will leave but a handful of descendents : the Aston-Martin Bulldog or Lagonda, the Sonic, the Nancy and other ill-known wonders created on behalf of mysterious backers. Still another section is devoted to the highly personalized creations of men of taste such as André Courrèges, Pierre Cardin and Walter Wolf.

Our favorite chapter is perhaps the one which recaps the talents of all those mentioned above. We have in fact entitled it "Talent and Technology." But enough said. Let the pictures speak for themselves. Let the pictures lead your imagination behind the wheel of a Sbarro or a Buchmann.

These road wonders were difficult to shoot for they were not long on display. Peter Vann had to show up each time before their proud owners hid them away beneath some slipcover in a garage somewhere in Phoenix, Arizona or near Clermont-Ferrand in central France.

As such, Peter Vann's images, highlighted by the technical contributions of Dirk Maxeiner, a foremost German automotive expert, make this much more than an ordinary car book.

Let this be a message of hope. As long as talented individuals continue to create such marvelous 4-wheeled (or 6-wheeled) objects; as long as they are able to induce fantasy among the visitors to drab auto shows where everything romantic has been banned, it will still be possible to dream on the policed, radar-watched and morose roads of our planet. If this book has a purpose, it is to encourage such men to keep up the good work and above all prevent us from waking up one morning to a world made functional through and through, in which vehicles which have provided us thousands of minutes of happiness are reduced to the status of a private subway car.

THE **Perfection**

CARUNA

The Sleek Price of Unobtrusive Beauty

An Austrian couple — man and wife — based in Zurich has found a market niche in converting already superb cars into custom specialties through almost imperceptible alterations. Their unobtrusive detailing yet results in something altogether different, starting with the price.

The thing costs 120,000 Swiss francs, meaning close to 50,000 US dollars. Yes, we're talking about the vehicle in the surrounding pictures. You may be thinking that for a Mercedes 280 S dressed up like this, such a price isn't terribly unreasonable. Except that the price doesn't include the basic car, just the Caruna modifications. Yup, $50,000 worth of customizing to make your beautiful sedan into a no less beautiful convertible. Still more amazing perhaps is that Mr. Erwin Schill, head of Caruna, maintains that he just can't meet the demand. It must be true too, since there's a six-month waiting list to get a Caruna.

So be it. Looking at Caruna's production rate, this is understandable: only 12 to 15 cars per year are output by Mr. and Mrs. Schill's shop. For this Swiss-naturalized Austrian, now based near Zurich, has chosen to work a family-type operation.

A war baby, Erwin Schill was in his twenties when he started "his business" in 1964. Specializing in custom sedans, he first applied his young entrepreneurial talents to Datsuns, Pontiacs and, later, to CX's, giving them a hatchback, for example, or providing a drawing table for the rear passengers! But the Schills' main line of work consists in creating original convertibles or "cabriolets" on a Porsche, Rolls or, especially, a Mercedes 280 S, 380 or 500 SE basis. If you like this V 126 model, you know what to do next: bring along your Mercedes and a check. The Schills will do the rest.

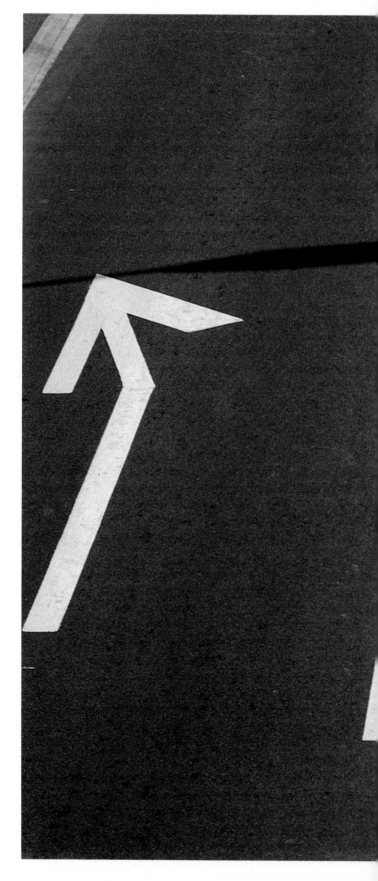

sts

Mercedes 280 S Caruna.

STYLING-GARAGE

Mercedes Cars for the Super-rich

This novel coachworks outfit based in Pinneberg, near Hamburg, has become a virtual supplier-to-the-court of the Arab royal houses.

"Is he allowed to do that?" asks a frightened child on his bicycle, staring through the opened gate of Styling-Garage where a man is busy slicing in half a gleaming new Mercedes 500 SE with a chain-saw. What the little boy doesn't know is that this number of sawing a Mercedes in half is actually a fine trick of magic. Within days, a new car will appear, having at least a meter of additional wheelbase and a full row of extra seats.

Upon investigation, Mercedes itself replies that, no, Styling-Garage is *not* allowed to do that. Christian Hahn, the head of the magic shop has in fact got an answer in writing: Daimler-Benz does not want to see the Mercedes star on the productions of Styling-Garage. Period. So it goes. Hahn has substituted his own symbol for the star. Nevertheless, customers with just a little curiosity will soon find a real three-point star in the glove compartment for subsequent fitting under their own responsibility.

Mercedes Management at Stuttgart keeps a suspicious eye on the Pinneberg firm's every move. And as Styling-Garage grows in fame, so also grows the mountain of summonses from Untertürkheim, for in less than two years the small workshop has become a large company specializing in the conversion of Mercedes. Several hundreds of the most costly and wildest Mercedes-Benzes have by now come out of Christian Hahn's styling shops. Oddly enough Hahn owes much of his success to Daimler-Benz itself. For each time an Arab prince requests a special touch for his Mercedes, such as a gold radiator grille or a longer wheelbase allowing the harem to lay back, Mercedes replies with polite firmness: "We don't make them."

The wealthy have known for ages however that everything has a price. That's why Mercedes enthusiasts who have been turned down by the venerable firm rush to Pinneberg, where they know wishes

will be fulfilled with a bright enthusiasm equal to their own — to Pinneberg, where in fact, anything goes. Having roughed it on the seven seas for ten years as a ship's officer, Christian Hahn is not easily taken aback. He listens unabashed as customers describe their most secret personal fantasies, ready, with his perfectly trained, specialized personnel to satisfy any demand.

Most customers find their knees turning to rubber on their first tour of the coachworks: there's gold agleam in one corner; elsewhere there's the almost overpowering scent of rich leather; or the dreamlike quality of good video and hi-fi. Here one can literally sink into the plush and fluff and luxuriate in a kaleidoscope of colors. It's the only bodyshop in the world where one might miss a mirror on the ceiling. It is a dreamland for even the wildest of dreams.

The most luxurious work yet accomplished by Styling-Garage was displayed at the Geneva Auto Show in 1983. The Garage so transformed a fiery red Mercedes 500 SE to suit the taste of an Arab client that the original car is hardly recognizable, its now giant wings hovering protectively over superb racing tires. Access to the cabin is through gullwing doors like those on the old Mercedes 300 SL. All the chromework of the original car has been plated with 24-carat gold. Altogether, the cost of materials alone came to 50,000 Marks — $18,000! The interior trim is all matching gold leather and every electronic plaything now on the market has been included, from an inboard computer to a telephone, to video and stereo system. There are more than 100 buttons and switches on the dashboard alone. And the stickshift knob is a gold falcon head with backlighted ruby eyes glowing in the dark.

The price tag on this golden machine is close to 350,000 Marks — roughly $120,000.

Christian Hahn knows how to live, and what's more, unlike many of his fellow car converters, he doesn't take himself all that seriously. As a rule he prefers good money to great praise. To Hahn, the customer is king... literally, as one of his recent orders for his team of 25 specialists proves: they were asked to make an entire fleet for a princely Arab wedding.

If you don't believe me, I'll swear before Allah that I saw these cars with my own eyes. There were several white Mercedes "G" models decorated with the rainbow colors of the sovereign's household, but destined to the staff. There were also two deluxe buses with the same color scheme, for the female employees, and finally a dozen matching Mercedes 500 SE coupes for the close relatives of the betrothed. The groom himself was provided with six such coupes, each in a different color: red, green, yellow, blue, black and white. The young man was to ride in a car of a different color each day of the week leading up to the wedding. (The Styling-Garage people have already repainted his Boeing, his helicopter and his yacht). Similarly color-matched motorcycles had to be prepared for the bodyguards accompanying the bridal procession. As a crowning touch, Styling-Garage built two actual nuptial carriages. The horses — all immaculately white, needless to say — were selected by Christian Hahn's own father, who owns a stable.

DUCHATELET CARAT

The Gold Star

Belgian body builder Duchatelet has provided the Mercedes 500 SE with a most luxurious livery. Even the Mercedes star is made of gold.

"Sorry, but I have already tripped the alarm", the inboard computer announces to a chance thief as soon as he settles into the driver's seat. As much as one and a half mile away, a beeper tells the owner that someone is preparing to make off with his gold gem without prior consent. This precautionary feature is indeed justified, since after all, the "Carat" is worth the price of a handsome estate, or nearly $120,000.

Obviously, at such a price, nothing that could contribute to the car's comfort has been left out. The beeper box, for example, also enables the owner to remote-start the engine and to preheat the passenger space to the desired temperature. Besides the quite expectable comforts of air conditioning, color television and telephone, the car has been provided with the ultimate in refinement for less visible details: the lighter is made of silver, the floor mats are sheepskin, and the seats are upholstered with the finest leather. There's also a liquor cabinet with silver tumblers from Cartier. And upon opening the small writing desk of exotic wood, you find two gold pens. Seen from the outside, the Carat differs from the Mercedes production model not only by its gold star, its new wheel rims and added chrome, but also by its paintwork: Instead of the usual seven coats, the Carat is given forty-eight (yes, 48!) coats of paint.

Rinspeed 939 Turbo.

RINSPEED

Made in Switzerland

Frank M. Rinderknecht, working out of his custom shop in Zurich, has specialized in customizing Volkswagens and Porsches.

Rinderknecht's hour of glory comes every year in springtime on the occasion of the Geneva Auto Show in which he has sworn to always be one of the stars. So far he's done alright. As a first entry, there's his very spectacular VW Golf that fits right in alongside a Ferrari or a Rolls. Up to the moment when you open the door ... upwards. Because Rinspeed has built the one-and-only Golf with gullwing doors. Also, the car has been endowed with all the best and the brightest of styling and accommodation. The passenger space, for one, has been literally moved out and replaced by a Porsche 928 interior. Quite appropriately, this Golf is trimmed with the finest leather and equipped with an almost mind-blowing stereo system blasting out 140 watt through as many as six speakers. The passenger can choose to watch the latest news on the car's tiny TV whilst savoring 20-year-old whisky from the liquor cabinet. Careful though! Lest the same passenger's necktie become a bib for splashing spirits as the Golf accelerates and the turbo kicks in at 4500 rpm, boosting the engine to its full 130 hp, steadily and irresistibly urging the vehicle on to a smooth-droning 125 mph. What pleasure for 100,000 Swiss francs!

The same amount of money would be a mere downpayment on Rinspeed's latest creation. It seems Rinspeed found a weakspot in the Porsche lineup where the new 911 cabriolet version hit the market minus the German company's most powerful engine — the 300 hp turbo. Rinspeed stepped right into the gap, fitting this engine into the rear of the car and producing one of the world's fastest convertibles. Gigantic rear spoilers have been added to keep the car from becoming airborne as it hits 155 mph. This is how things must have been in the cockpit of one of those old fighter planes. When you step off the gas the exhaust sputters like a machinegun. Rather than showing his license to a traffic cop, the proud

owner of a "Rinspeed 939" should perhaps stand on his right to bear arms. As it goes though, at 300,000 Swiss francs or thereabouts, there won't be many to make that claim.

In a more pastoral repertory, Rinspeed also offers a version of the Suzuki ST 410, a compact 4×4 (13.77 in. long by 59 in. wide), that is highly popular in the Swiss mountains. A very stylish car, this "pink panther" with aggressive paws knows how to protect itself through a whole array of devices. Last but not least, its many chromium trims look defiantly at current trends.

Rinspeed Golf Aliporta.

WOOD & PICKETT

Distinctive English Style

Wood & Pickett is a big among the small, since it has been founded in 1947 by Bill Wood and Les Pickett. The firm's success is mainly due to the fact that it has built a proud reputation on its custom bodies and luxurious interior fittings.

The cowl does make the monk! And it's a shame that today's production cars as a rule are poorly dressed. The great plastic tide has reached as high as Mercedes and BMW. Sure, the interior trim is now washable and easy to maintain, but there's no personality left in production cars. They're soulless and about as kinky as a refrigerator. So it feels good to see those old English cars with their impeccably polished woodwork, their splenndid, round meter dials, their Conolly leather and solid chrome door handles which are altogether a sight for the sore eyes of a discriminating enthusiast. Luckily enough, any new-car owner with a penchant for the past is welcome to have his car retro-processed at Wood & Pickett's. The workforce there is still British and hasn't forgotten its know-how. The W & P team will put patience and the richest materials together to breathe new charm and glory into production's dullest bodies. It deserves extra praise for taking an interest even in very small, unglamorous cars and has in fact produced the nicest and costliest Minis of all time. Yes, these guardians of tradition have dressed both the Mini and her sister, the Metro, for the ball.

The look of the Laser Metro has been definitely improved through mere alterations to the grille, safety bumpers, wheel rims with P7 tires, and spoilers. Naturally, the engine is turbocharged. In General, Wood & Pickett are still working mainly on British automobiles. Rovers are given more specific attention: the Rover 3500 is one of the firm's flagships, but the top best-sellers are a 2-door, convertible Range Rover (the Sheer Rover) and a beautiful, 4-door, convertible Range Rover with wheelbase extended by 9.85 in.

The most celebrated W & P is the Mini Margrave, an odd little British Leyland whose rear windows have almost disappeared to take on a Landaulet style.

However, the most dramatic Wood & Pickett (today, even in London, there is a "show-off car" market) is a 6-wheeled, hugely extended Range Rover. An enormous "buffalo-guard" completes the car's aggressive look. A car that looks however designed to travel Hyde Park Lane and Berkeley Square rather than the Kenyan reservation tracks. But, as we've said before, the British definitely like to turn aside from the beaten track.

Taking the lead in Great Britain in the field of customizing or converting is no doubt a feat in a country where, from Lotus to Morgan, from Aston Martin to Bristol, it appears that a whole population of aficionados stubbornly turns aside from the beaten track of the automotive world.

Sheer Rover
Metro Laser ▶

38

PININFARINA

This little man is the greatest.

Fifty years ago, a nickname became a marque of world reknown. Battista Farina, known as Pinin — the "kid" — because of his small stature, founded his own coachwork shop. His son, Sergio, has taken up the reins, and ensures the firm's continuing success.

Little men tend to do great things — just look at all those Napoleons who want to take Moscow at any price. And there are the others, who have bequeathed great achievements to posterity. Battista Farina, for example, was just 5 ft high, and the greatest coachbuilder of all time. He came from a peasant family, born in Turin in 1893, the very year Carl Benz brought out his first mass-produced car, the "Victoria".

The tenth child in a family of eleven children, Farina did not have a very comfortable youth. "Take longer strides", his mother used to say, "you'll wear your shoes down less." Having learnt that lesson very young, he made giant steps in his career: 4 years of elementary schooling, then a mechanic's apprentice, at 17, he met Fiat's founder, Agnelli, for whom he designed his first car. It can be seen today in the Turin Automobile Museum.

Pininfarina XJ spider.

From then on, his star never stopped rising. Farina became a car designer, something quite new in those days. Even Henry Ford, the automobile tycoon at the time, wanted to hire Farina. But Pinin refused. In 1930, Farina founded his own coachwork shop.

Since then no one has been so successful in designing today's car. The Italian Government shared that view, since in 1961, five years before Farina's death, they authorized him to use the surname "Pininfarina".

Today his son Sergio and his son-in-law Renzo Carli run the Pininfarina business which remains the best automobile "couture" address. The factory's operations include four divisions, in particular body-work styling for car manufacturers, as well as finished prototype projects. For rich private customers they build one-off models, and for the car industry, whole series of bodies. About 25 million cars have been built either in the workshops or by builder-customers following Pininfarina designs. Still, the most dramatic achievements are self-financed designs. In Motor Shows the world over, they display the Italian genius. One of them, the Cisitalia 1945, is exhibited today in New York's Museum of Modern Art, as "Sculpture in Movement".

Pininfarina and his heirs designed most Ferraris, a good many Alfa-Romeos, Fiats, Lancias and Peugeots. They have worked for BMW and DKW and have been consultants to Daimler Benz and Volkswagen. They also created the most expensive mass-produced car in the world: the Rolls-Royce Camargue, and contributed to the most legendary small car: the Austin Mini.

When Pininfarina still worked on his own drawing-board, he signed his own work with a small blue "f" topped by a crown. Journalists often asked him if he found inspiration in the female body. Pininfarina answered: "Perhaps from the point of view of the architecture of a woman's body, yes... but a woman's beauty is a moment in time, something that cannot be put down on paper."

The great coachbuilder himself admitted to a greater influence by his friend Vicenzo Lancia. "Go to the mountains in winter, and see how the wind carves out the snow and the landscape," advised Lancia. Pininfarina soon realized that beautiful shapes went hand in hand with the wind. Indeed, the wind slips easily and effortlessly over Pininfarina's streamlined creations.

The 1970 Modulo has been a smashing example

of a self-financed achievement. The dream car was built on the most astounding basis at the time: the Ferrari 512 S, a racing car of which only 25 units had been built. Its clean lines made of modular components were — and still are — quite as astounding.

Even today, all the firm's products are characterized by their outstanding aerodynamics. Nothing surprising about that, since, as early as 1972, Pininfarina inaugurated the first wind-tunnel in Italy, while in comparison, General Motors, the biggest car manufacturer in the world, only acquired a wind-tunnel in 1980. Even if the great are close on the heels of the small, they didn't manage to overtake him yet.

Sergio, the son, put the idea of a wind-tunnel into practice : it was a favourite dream of his : "Even when I was just a student, it was a passion of mine, always in the back of my mind. The idea of the struggle against the elements... A well drawn line offers wind noise, better road-holding in case of side-winds, lighter bodywork and better performance for the same fuel consumption." But he does not believe that, because the wind-tunnel is in use, all cars will look the same in the future. "Creative minds will always find a way to produce original cars with a distinct personality. We have all kinds of techniques available. Not just shaping, but colours, the way we work our materials, window alterations, air-intakes and outlets that are more or less elaborate, can make a car that stands out in a crowd," says Sergio Pininfarina.

The Pininfarina XJ spider produced in 1978 is another self-financed, outstanding achievement as it kept up, with its skillfully updated lean lines and shark nose, the somewhat lost tradition of the Type D and E Jaguars. Year after year, the Pininfarina XJ remains timelessly distinctive, and that's the reason why John Egan, jaguar's new boss, fell in love with it. A version slightly altered for mass-production will soon appear in the market. All Jaguar aficionados can expect the car for the year 1986. This sports car, which tops at 150 mph, should also be available in a coupé version. Naturally, the powerplant will be the smooth-running 285-hp, 12 cylinder engine.

With the Audi Quartz, a 2 + 2 coupé based on the 4-wheel-drive Audi Quattro, Pininfarina not only wanted to prove that a car can be streamlined while having a character of its own, but above all that the use of new lightweight materials derived from space

research meant new body designs. He says that you cannot just replace heavy materials with light ones, because the properties of modern materials like Kevlar, Honeycomb, or carbon fiber, or metal and plastic laminates are far too complex. A whole new rethink is needed in terms of technique and style to find innovative solutions: one component is enough where five were needed previously.

Still in the field of new product and new style research, Pininfarina displayed at the 1983 Geneva Auto Show a four-seater, sports coupé based on the Fiat Ritmo Abarth 125 TC. This project, which definitely favors roominess — a feature often underestimated in coupés — is not intended to remain single: it will be produced under the Pininfarina marque. Thus, it will provide 4-wheeled proof of Pininfarina's assertion: Modern cars do not have to be all the same. Actually, he is even convinced that the glorious years of car stylists are yet to come: "The car is a product that evolves at a tremendous rate; apart from a few historic steps forward, this is what typifies a young product.

Fiat Ritmo Abarth 125 TC.

BERTONE

Style and Tradition

In the realm of dream cars, Bertone is a king. His factory not only produces unique curios intended for auto shows, but also mass production dream cars for Mr. Everyman. The most significant example is the little Fiat 850 Spider designed by Bertone, which was a 140,000 car best-seller. However, in spite of such industrial dimension, the Bertone team never lost its taste for the outstanding. Thus, a small designer group separate from the factory, the "Stile Group", is in charge of designing prototypes and show cars.

The draftsmen, designers, engineers, model makers, technicians and workers making up the Bertone "Stile Group" are totally independent from the parent factory located in Caprie, some fifteen miles from Turin — an address well known to major automakers. Renault, Jaguar, Alfa Romeo, Volkswagen, Fiat, BMW, and many others who go unnamed, come and fetch ideas there. These auto-

Lamborghini Marzal.

Lancia Stratos HF.

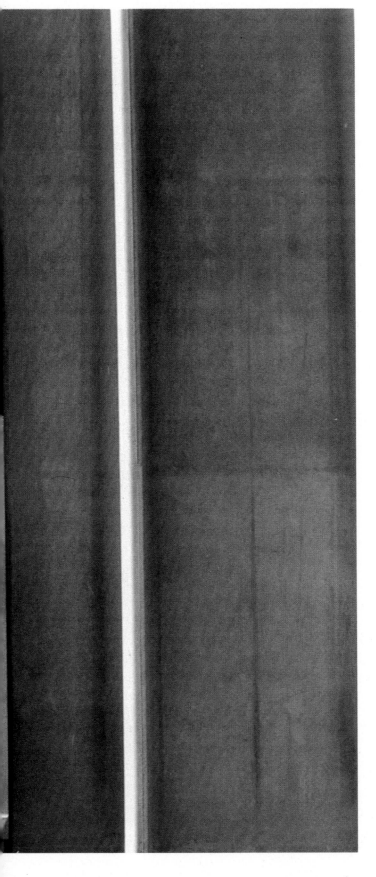

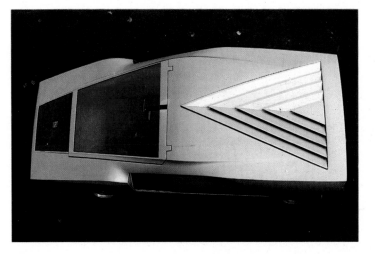

makers may order a full prototype as well as a detail for a car: an instrument panel, rims or seats, for example. Italians are well known for their top-quality work, and for working fast as well. Thus, the first Volkswagen Polo — a Bertone design, indeed — was completed within forty-five days only... A record which major automobile groups cannot even dream of!

But the Bertone staff is still bent on dreaming, and this is the reason why they show a marked preference for the firm's own orders. Mostly, they will design the car that will make a sensation in an auto show, without worrying about price or client requirements. "So, they remain in high spirits", says

"who enjoy total contact with nature", Bertone says, and who therefore "accept with youthful enthusiasm the inconveniences due to bad weather, just as motorcyclists do". As far as the car's lines are

Lancia Sibilo.

concerned, the Master says that «the proportions of the Athon tend to back-up the mechanical performance efficiency of the engine". Moreover, the Athon — a name derived from Ancient Egypt's sun worship — is not only open in terms of body, but also in terms of price. As a matter of fact, not for the world and certainly not for 400,000 dollars would Bertone part with it. Actually, the specimen is now displayed in the firm's gallery of automotive masterpieces. Says a Bertone employee with respect to all those masterpieces: "It would be a pity to see it crash land in a tree, in the hands of a millionaire".

The preliminary project of the 1970 Lancia "Stratos" is even farther from reality. At the time, Lancia had asked Bertone to design a sports car epitomizing "a totally novel concept". The project came out to Lancia's expectations... Actually, the Stratos was more of a flying saucer than a car. Bertone had given a free hand to his designers; that is why,

Lamborghini Athon.

powerplant, the low-slung, silver gray coupe reaches a top speed of 137 mph. Last but not least, the Delfino is quite suitable for family use, since it can accommodate two adults, two teenagers, plus their luggage.

among other peculiarities, the driver needed to fold back the windscreen to get into the car. For daily use, this was naturally a bit too much, and Bertone reshaped his initial project which resulted in the Lancia Stratos we can see today.

While the midrear engine coupe that became famous for its rally-winning record, had two doors which are quite conventional today, it was still classy enough to push its rivals into the background.

Recently, Bertone designed a new coupe based on the Alfa Romeo "Alfa 6" sedan. His Delfino is a successful combination of a rugged body and aerodynamic lines. The Delfino's headlamps are retractable in the daytime, and all-round glass eliminates blind angles. With its 6-cylinder, 157-hp Alfa

Alfa Romeo Delfino

78

Talent and

SBARRO

Masterpieces for Wealthy Enthusiasts

Italian Franco Sbarro's dream of having his own small auto factory finally came true across the border, in Switzerland. Sbarro has been nicknamed "the master of replica" for his unmatched ability to revive splendid oldies with all the advantages of modern technology. Meanwhile, not having any particular dislike of modernism, he offers what may be the world's most amazing car range.

The (true) tale doesn't mention vilains or victims, but it's clear that a happy ending is at hand, thanks to a man named Sbarro. As the story goes, a rich Mercedes 500 owner (it's pleonastic, sorry...), having found the options offered by Stuttgart altogether "unexciting", came to see a craftsman to have his car more astoundingly arranged. The bodyman suggested a recreation of a gullwing coupe. He altered, cut up the body, and, delighted with the quite visible results, the owner drove off with a dashing new machine. On returning home, unfortunately, he was unpleasantly surprised to find the door he just slammed still in his hands. Furious to see his brilliant idea falling into spare parts, the enthusiast decided to investigate and discovered that only one man — Sbarro — could save what remained of the car and fulfill his dream. Just looking at the photos of the gullwing door Sbarro Mercedes on these pages, you can see that Sbarro hasn't usurped his reputation as a one-man design band.

That the cream of car lovers would one day queue up at his door is one thing Franco Sbarro, the farmer's son, wouldn't have dared even to dream some twenty-seven years ago, as he mugged up for examinations in the small Italian town of Lecce while devoting his spare time to becoming a self-taught auto mechanic. "All I wanted", he recalls now, at age 44, "was to keep busy with something relating to automobiles".

Shahin 1000.

Technology

THE LOLA T 70 REPLICA

The Lola T 70 first appeared on race tracks in 1967 and, since then, has come to be considered one of the most beautiful racing cars of all time, achieving an ideal combination of style and technology. In its time, the T 70 was fast enough to upstage the powerful Porsche 917 from the Stuttgart-Zuffenhausen factory. Some time ago, the builder of the T 70, Briton Eric Broadley, came to call on Franco Sbarro and asked him: "build me a T 70 for the road". A year later, Sbarro had delivered his little wonder — in British Racing Green livery, *bien sûr*. The car's remarkable construction and finishing

quickly made it a prime focus of conversation among initiates. Meanwhile, Sbarro had put as many as twelve T 70 replicas on wheels, pricing them in the neighborhood of 170,000 Swiss francs per bombshell, depending on the customer-designated engine used. To Sbarro's great regret, a good number of customers rejected the original Chevrolet V8 engine in favor of an alien powerhouse. Thus, one of these T 70's roars to the 12-cylinder tune of a Ferrari engine, while another purrs along with a 3.3-liter Porsche Turbo. Yet, differ as they might in terms of sound, all these T 70 replicas have one significant common attribute: breathtaking performance. According to Sbarro, their top speed is better than 186 mph; obviously the T 70's long, streamlined bodying plays no small part in this. There's one minus in all the pluses though: the car is tough on large customers. Tall drivers will have to perform a certain amount of gymnastics to get inside as the driver's space is extremely low and narrow; and visibility through the sides and the rear is quite limited. Actually, the Sbarro T 70 is to auto buffs somewhat as a desirable woman: beautiful but trying.

THE SBARRO TAG

Akram Ojjeh, a petrodollar billionaire from the Middle East, has a predilection for ocean liners. He thus made newspaper headlines when he bought himself the « France » for the spritely sum of 1.2 billion dollars. His second liner doesn't sail the seven seas, however, but merely cruises the streets of Geneva. This mobile office of a car from TAG (short for "Techniques d'Avant-Garde" makes Mr. Ojjeh's trips from the airport to the hotel or the bank all the less trying. The car's heavy, 660 lbs, armored rear door opens onto — of all things — an actual conference room. Its walls are agleam with posh walnut veneer and there are four vast armchairs inviting guests to extend their stay. Passengers may also bask in stereo music unfurling from a high-tech sound system, or catch their favorite movies on the videotape player. The only hint a passenger might have of moving down the road is a slight shifting of the TAG's body from time to time. The chauffeur works out of sight, behind an opaque glass partition. He also works unheard, as does the 8-cylinder Cadillac engine driving the front wheels — the rear wheels serving only to evenly distribute the vehicle's three tons. The chauffered passenger, feeling rushed, need only notify the driver via the intercom. Brisk driving will bring tears of emotion to the eyes of Arab potentates: the 6.9-liter, 8-cylinder powerhouse gayly guzzles a good 14 gallons every 100 miles just like in the good old days. The TAG — an OPEC dream car!

THE SBARRO WINDHAWK

"I need a special car for hawking". Thus spoke Saudi King Khalid once upon a time to Franco Sbarro. The King was bothered by having to get out of his car time and time again while hunting. Sbarro therefore began by looking up the "how to's" of falconry, then went to work at his drawing board.

Two days later all the basic roughs for the Windhawk were on paper. Henceforth, thanks to a fully-opening roof, the King can loose his hawk to flight without leaving his car. To ensure that he won't lose sight of the hawk, a hydraulic lift is provided to raise the seats 30 inches above roof-level. This all-wheel drive, six-wheeled huntmobile further enables longer outings due to a 92-gallon gas tank and a 40-gallon fresh water tank. Ground clearance

can be increased from 10 to 16 1/2 inches through a second hydraulic system. With a top speed of 124 mph made possible by its 214-hp Mercedes engine, the Windhawk has little to envy in its real, feathered namesake. The engine was the only mandatory requirement imposed on Sbarro. "It *must* come from Mercedes", said the King. It should be mentioned that this monarch has a very special predilection for cars made by the Stuttgart firm. His automobile fleet comprises more than 100 cars, of which 90% are Mercedes. The birds of prey themselves are impressed by the comfort of this newest-born Mercedes: the chunks of meat fed to them as a reward come straight from the inboard fridge!

THE GOLF TURBO

It takes just a light push on a lever to drop the chassis and hydraulically raise the back of the "Sbarro-Porsche Golf." At which point the broad rear hatch of this sheet-metal oyster discloses such a pearl as has never been seen in the back of a Golf: a 345-hp Porsche Turbo engine. This arrangement is very convenient for working on the engine, notes the inventor. "What's more," he adds, grinning, "you can get such a thrill flashing a raised tail at the cars left standing at the light." But the realm of the Golf Turbo is hardly one of traffic light crossings — far from it. Actually it's out on the highway, where the Sbarro-tweaked black GTi leaves even its real Porsche Turbo sisters in the dust. The Golf's top speed is about 165 mph.

Seen from the outside on the other hand, the car is most discreet. Its modest black body features an air intake on each side; its tires are a bit wider, but not unusual for a GTi, with 195/15 at the front and 225/15 at the back. And speaking of the back, that's where the maker's name appears in generously

THE SUPER TWELVE

Ok, so it doesn't fly! But among four-wheel dwarfs, the Super Twelve is still Superman. Strong, bold and what a heart! The first compact built by Sbarro, as its name implies, has twelve cylinders, or more accurately, two times six inline. As each 1.3-liter, 6-cylinder Kawasaki motorcycle engine in the set generates 118 horsepower, the Super Twelve actually has 236 hp available. Given the car's mini proportions (10 feet long, 1760 lbs), the result is an unbeatable power-to-weight ratio. Compared with the Porsche Turbo's horses, which must each pull 9.7 lbs, the Super Twelve's horses need only haul 7.2 lbs apiece. This is why, when the green light comes and the Super Twelve takes off, all the other cars seem to be parked. In just eight seconds, the Super will be going at 100 miles, at 8000 rpm. The two engines generally begin with a gurgle, but they end the acceleration with a bellow like a pack of bulls.

The Kawasakis, each with its own transmission, are laid out side-by-side, transversally, ahead of the rear axle. The two five-speed gearboxes are worked via a common lever and two transmission linkages. Power is applied to the rear wheels through a chain set. Sbarro couldn't see any use for a differential, so the two engines are simply coupled by V-belts which help to compensate variations in torque. And there's a final feature unique to this two-engine design: if for any reason one of the two should go on strike, the other engine is quite capable of

spaced letters: S b a r r o. As hinted at previously, the engine is lodged where the rear seat goes in a normal Golf, while in the space provided for the normal Golf's engine — at the front of the car — Franco Sbarro has fitted a 25-gallon fuel tank. The weight distribution in a car with two occupants is thus a virtually ideal 50/50. The owner, a Swiss industrialist, need not worry about his add-on rear chassis going its own way after the engine starts because the engine is secured safely to the rest of the frame by hydraulic muscles exerting some 7 tons of pressure to keep everything together.

hauling the Super Twelve as far as the nearest Kawasaki repair shop.

All the instruments except the speedometer have been doubled up, one for each engine. The interior decoration is all leather and brown velour. Space-wise, the dwarf will accommodate two adults, plus two children if required. And the front seats —

Recaros — can be backed off so far that even a 6'3" giant will be comfortable.

The base though, betrays the racing car penchant of the builder. It consists of a tubular frame and front and rear axles connected by a rigid center tube. The rear wheel suspension is absolutely unique. Simpflifying to the utmost, Sbarro has used the

drive chain housings as suspension arms for the wheels, with damping being provided by two MacPherson struts. Front and rear disk brakes are provided in an attempt to bridle this spritely elf.

In keeping with Sbarro tradition, the body is of carefully engineered plastic. The front fenders arc over 196/50 tires; the bulbous rear wings harbor slightly larger, 235/70 × 16 tires. These are Pirelli P7's. Finally, as if this weren't enough to make the Super Twelve quite noticeable, Sbarro has dressed it up in rather surprising livery: stunningly white at the front going to increasing by deep shades of red as you move to the back. This hot-tempered imp is priced at nearly 120,000 Swiss francs.

B + B

An Idea Factory

As a student, Rainer Buchmann managed to buy himself a Porsche as a result of repairing other Porsches. His tiny repair shop has now become a real idea factory.

In 1973, young Rainer Buchmann from Frankfurt rented a small workshop at the back of a courtyard and founded the "b + b" company with the aim of upgrading Porsches. "Only a fool or an idiot would launch out into the automobile industry right in the middle of the oil crisis" — these were the kind of mocking comments that could be heard at the time from the lips of so-called tradespeople. However, Buchmann had learnt the lessons of the mechanical engineering, management and psychology courses attended and had come to quite an opposed conclusion. "The oil crisis is our best chance of succeeding. If you are no loger allowed to drive faster than the others, then you want to be marked off in any other way." In other words: nothing resists a crisis better than snobbery.

Today, ten years later, facts show that Rainer Buchmann was right. In that rather short time, he has turned his tuning workshop into a small — but splendid — idea factory that even major automakers take seriously. Clients like BMW of Volkswagen can bear witness to that.

However, it was a long way to get up there. And to travel it in such a short period of time, Buchmann had to devote an enormous amount of energy to the project. Several important stages marked his astounding rise:

1973:
Buchmann began by upgrading Porsche models. Not that he gave them more powerful engines (the Porsches are already richly endowed with horsepower) but instead he offered different paintwork and high-class fittings to his well-to-do clients. The gilded instrument panel, which is not available from Porsche, is an example. At Buchmann's, both prices and ideas have no bounds.

1976/77:
Little by little, Buchmann hired skilled manpower. Thus, he took on Manuel Melero, on out-of-work bullfighter of remarkable dexterity. With a hammer and a suresighted eye as his only tools, he can hand-turn perfectly curved new metal sheeting. He learnt that skill in Spain, at a time there was spare parts shortage in the Iberian peninsula. For Buchmann, such a talent opened up entirely new prospects. So, one day, a black Porsche Turbo attracted the attention of the international automobile press. The front looked like a Porsche 928, the middle ressembled a Targa and the rear looked like a

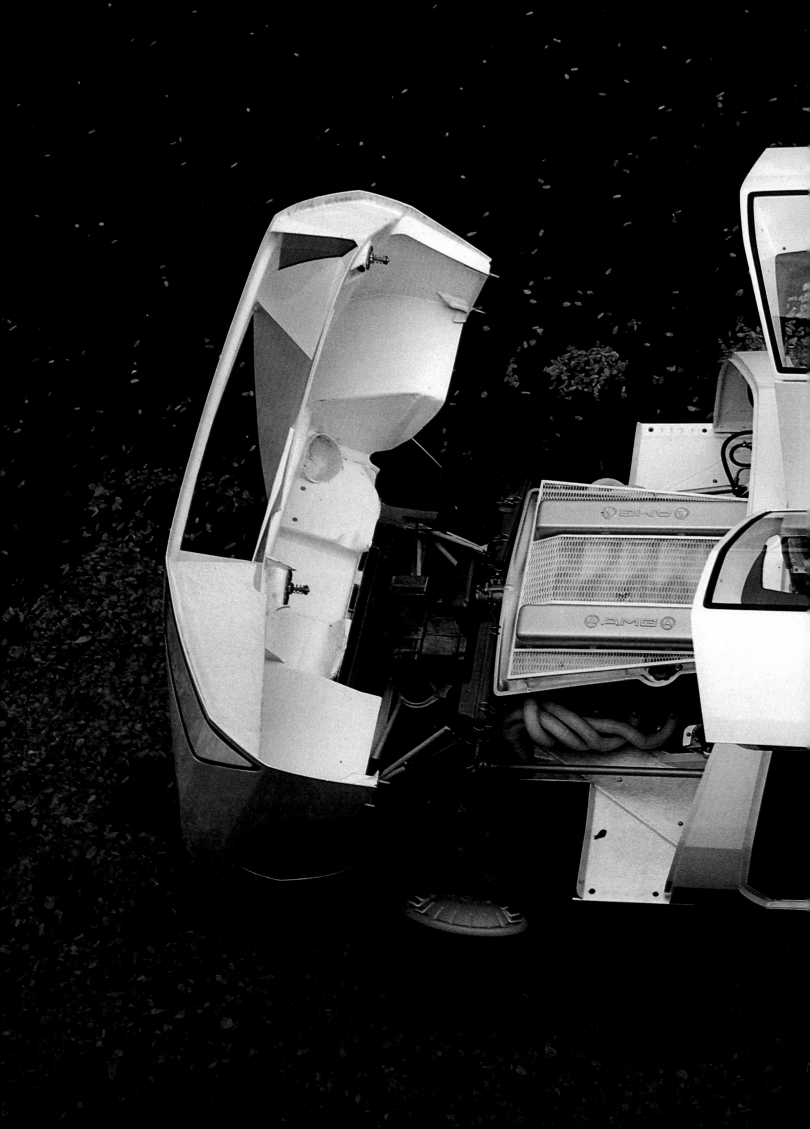

Turbo. The car was sold in 1977 to a buyer in Curaçao for 250,000 Deutsche marks, or about 80,000 dollars. By the way, the Caribbean island has only 2 miles of freeway. The client, a gambling club owner, also had a magnum gun fitted under the seat as an accessory.

1978:

The breakthrough. Buchmann has just found the right man at the right time. Eberhard Schulz, who was 37 at the time and had felt that seven years spent at the drawing-board in the Porsche factory was quite long enough, went to see Buchmann with the final project of the CW 311 in his briefcase.

B+B Turbo

Khalid ordered the car).

In addition to the customizing business, "b + b" initiated a second activity in 1978 — Electronics. That year the two partners decided to develop the electronic instrument panel "Dinfos" (Digital Information System).

At the time, Buchmann wanted to be taken more seriously in the field of research, since until then the major automakers had merely tolerated his activities. In the beginning, his customizing jobs were greeted with scorn by Porsche; even Mercedes displayed amused scepticism. Then came the truce when BMW gave Buchmann the job of designing the "Futuro" motorcycle.

The fuss made about the Futuro eventually brought Buchmann his most important client so far. Volkswagen asked him to fit his Dinfos instrument panel to a limited series of Polos, for research purposes. In the meantime, Buchmann had already demonstrated the capabilities of his LEDs through research performed on the Golf.

The electronic facia has three displays providing the driver with any information he could possibly need. The left display shows speed, mileage and fuel level. The one in the middle gives at the push of a

B + B Polo Paris.

LANCIA

LANCIA RALLY

Comeback of the Supercharger

With the Rally model, Lancia remembered the glorious pre-war days and dug up the Supercharger.

Lancia has no intention of turning its Rally into a commercial success. Actually, production has been limited to 200 units — just enough to get rally approval. The only trace left of the original Monte-Carlo it is derived from is the passenger's seat. Everything else in the Rally has been restyled by a successfully inspired Pininfarina. The front and rear are each made up of a single, easy-to-disassemble plastic unit. The open-air engine fitted beneath the rear window displays its technical assets. This time, the in-line four-cylinder engine is not charged with air from a turbocharger but breaths through a plain old supercharger instead. The Roots unit being mechanically actuated by the first kick of the engine, thus provides fairly good horsepower even at low rev. The new powerplant puts out 200 hp, and over 315 in the racing version.

Achievement

Lamborghini Countach.

LAMBORGHINI

The Heart of a Fighting Bull

One factory in the small Italian town of Sant'Agata Bolognese has been regularly producing sports cars whose top speeds compare with those usually associated with Formula One cars. Yet despite a loyal following of customers throughout the world, this factory had run into serious financial difficulties. Today, with its new boss, 26-year-old Patrick Mimran, the factory is coming back into the black.

Young Mimran, a Frenchman of Lebanese origin, graduated from the University of Geneva, then rounded out his education in a Swiss bank in accordance with papa's wishes. Having pleased his father, he asked him one day: "Would you buy me

— Lamborghini's flagship car — is again being produced at a rate of several units weekly. The motor world can thank Patrick Mimran for saving the Countach — one of the most astounding sports cars of all time — from going out of production.

Indeed, although the basic design of this flounder dates back to 1971, the car's attractiveness hasn't been diminished in the least by its more than ten years of existence. It should be emphasized that Nuccio Bertone really outdid himself with this one: even at a standstill, the Countach looks faster than many of the competitors at 155 mph.

Twelve cylinders, 4.8-liter displacement, four overhead camshafts, six dual crossdraft Weber carburetors. Horsepower: 370 hp at 8000 rpm. Top speed: 185 mph. Pickup to 100 mph in 8.3 seconds, or 200 mph in 29 seconds. Dry sump lubrication takes 4 gallons of oil. The two fuel tanks, which like the engine and the transmission, are located at the midrear of the vehicle, take up to 32 gallons of fuel. The starter itself, a 1.8 hp design, is as powerful as a motorbike...

The handmade aluminum body conceals a rather complex tubular frame which is both extremely stiff and lightweight. The Countach weighs some 2866 lbs, which is in fact not much for such a gauge of car. The power-to-weight ratio comes out to 7.7 lbs/hp, even with air conditioning, stereo radio and luxury leather trim inside.

The front and rear wishbone suspension gives away the Countach's racing car origins. The front tires are 205/50s and the rear tires are 345/35s.

It's lunch hour and there are too many cars on the road from Sant'Agata to Castelfranco Emilia. Pietro Borgo, Lamborghini's test driver, suggests that we'd be better off on the highway. I'm feeling insecure: I can't see anything out the rear and, in the front, the car stops at the windshield.

But once on the highway, even glance in the rearview mirror becomes useless. I shift up through the gears. My body is plastered to the seat, my arms and legs feel heavy; I'm breathing hard. I'm on a trip to hell. Anyone with a whim to follow us would need a small jet plane from here on. I'm driving at 185 mph for the first time in my life! The Countach is swallowing 90 yards of road every second. We have only one concern vis-à-vis the other cars on the road: please, don't any of you switch lanes...

We return to the factory for a short visit of the

Lamborghini?" The elder Mimran, a more-than-wealthy businessman, wasn't even ruffled. Just for the record, he asked: "How much does the car cost?" And Patrick quickly corrected: "It's not the car I want, but the factory." Papa caught his breath but just as quickly took out his wallet, and that's how Patrick Mimran became the new head of Lamborghini just when the latter was heading for bankruptcy. And he, whom company insiders call "the kid," has succeeded in accomplishing what no one thought possible: he is turning Lamborghini around.

Exports show an upwards trend and the Countach

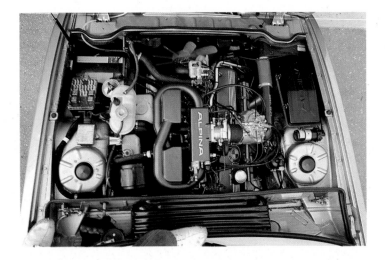

Obviously, the transmission and suspension also now require major surgery. In addition to the 5-speed the B7 Coupe is equipped with more powerful ventilated front disc brakes. The differential gets its own cooling system cum radiator and fluid pump. The progressive suspension and Bilstein gas-pressure dampers combine with a set of different-sized wheels and tires to provide secure footing. The front tires are 205/55 VR 16's and the rear tires are 225/VR 16's. The rear wheel rims also have a slightly greater diameter. This rather unobtrusive B7 Coupe even compares quite favorably with the best sports cars in terms of performance: 0-100 mph in 9.6 seconds; top speed above 155 mph.

RENAULT

R5 TURBO

A Wolf in Lamb's Clothes

With its Renault 5 Turbo, the French government-owned automaker has produced a no-compromise rally car. That's what makes the car such a thrill to drive in normal road traffic.

The Renault engineers put their usual trade-off mind on the back burner as soon as Management gave them the go-ahead to build a future rally-winner. They converted the front wheel drive design to rear wheel drive; they moved the engine from front to behind the driver's seat; and they cut back on seating from five to two. As for the trunk, it was hocus-pocussed right out of existence. Even the road version, with its turbocharged 140-hp, 1.4-liter engine and light weight (2140 lbs), performs amazingly. This R5 handles like a go-kart. A skillful driver can skid it through corners in the grand style of rally drivers. All he'll need is a little guts and a bit extra rubber... Given a good mastery of the 5-speed gearbox, you can get to 100 mph in 11.1 seconds. Top speed is limited to 127 mph though, due to a not-so-favorable drag coefficient. Actually, the wind has some trouble getting past those rather bulky, built-up fenders. Which of course is not a problem in rallying since speeds higher than 105 mph are rarely required. Good handling and quick acceleration on the other hand are essential, as is ease of access to mechanical parts. It takes the Renault rally team mechanics only 90 minutes to replace the engine and transmission.

Driving the R5 Turbo on winding roads or in the mountain is sheer fun. Provided the "modest" Porsche or Jaguar driver before you admits to be left far behind by a small Renault 5.

From Unit To Very

ASTON MARTIN LAGONDA

70 Years On And Still A Maverick!

The British factory building Aston Martin Lagonda sports cars is one of the oldest established in the field. Its 70-year old history is full of ups and downs. Despite never-ending financial problems, these British persist in building some of the fastest, most exclusive cars in the world.

If you pass through the small market town of Newport Pagnell, two hours' drive from London, you go straight through the middle of the Aston Martin factory! On either side of the highway, you can see the old brick buildings where "Astons" are still hand-built. There's nowhere else in the world where cars are built in such idyllic surroundings. Everyone takes his time at Aston Martin. Even today, one single craftsman builds his own engine.

Continuity is the key-word at Newport Pagnell — They have been in the business for the last 70 years. The factory was founded in 1913 by a garage mechanic, Lionel Martin, who had just won the Aston Clinton hill climb. Beside himself with joy, he christened the firm with its new trademark "Aston Martin". From that time on, the firm has had its ups and downs. At one time, it even took the name "R & B Specials" — Not a very auspicious name. Things changed in 1947 when David Brown took over Aston Martin and the firm Lagonda for the paltry price of 52,000 pounds.

By dogged hard work, he turned the small firm into one of the most celebrated sports car makers in the world. The DB Series became increasingly powerful, with the 6-cylinder, 3.7 litre DB4 in 1959 generating 240 hp.

It was a secret agent by the name of James Bond, alias "007", who brought their crowning glory. In the film "Goldfinger", the hero made his way through enemy ground in an Aston Martin DB 5. He was forewarned of danger by the car's built-in radar system, and if, despite these precautions, a

Aston Martin Lagonda Bulldog.

Limited Production

baddie managed to get into the passenger seat, an ejector seat sent him promptly flying into space.

Things were not much better for pursuers. When it was not a machine gun firing from the rear of the car, it was a vicious oil slick that turned the highway into a skating rink. If, in spite of that, the killers reappeared, knife-blades emerged from the wheel-hubs to chop their tires into little pieces.

Even if Aston Martins no longer carry that sort of option, this does not mean those British have become any more sensible. In 1976, Aston Martin had creditors at their heels once again, like killers at James Bond's heels, and yet they designed their own version of the car for the year 2000. This bombshell named "Lagonda" is perhaps the fastest moving escape route known to man. A powerful 4-door sedan, and lines uncompromisingly drawn by English stylist William Towns. With its 208 in. long, it

is not far short of a Cadillac. Following the motto "No expense spared", the Lagonda weighs a full two tons.

The interior is as futuristic as the body. Digital display electronic instruments, which in 1976 were fitted on no other mass-produced car, keep the driver informed. Actually, the dashboard LEDs did not work properly right away: Technicians had to work on them for a further two years before things were like clockwork, to the great displeasure of those customers who had bought tomorrow's car on the spur of the moment. Nobody likes to be kept waiting two years for his new toy to be delivered, especially when the toy costs well over 30,000 pounds.

But let us forget those teething troubles. Today, LEDs show speed, revs, fuel level and everything the driver wishes to know. Of course, the rest of the

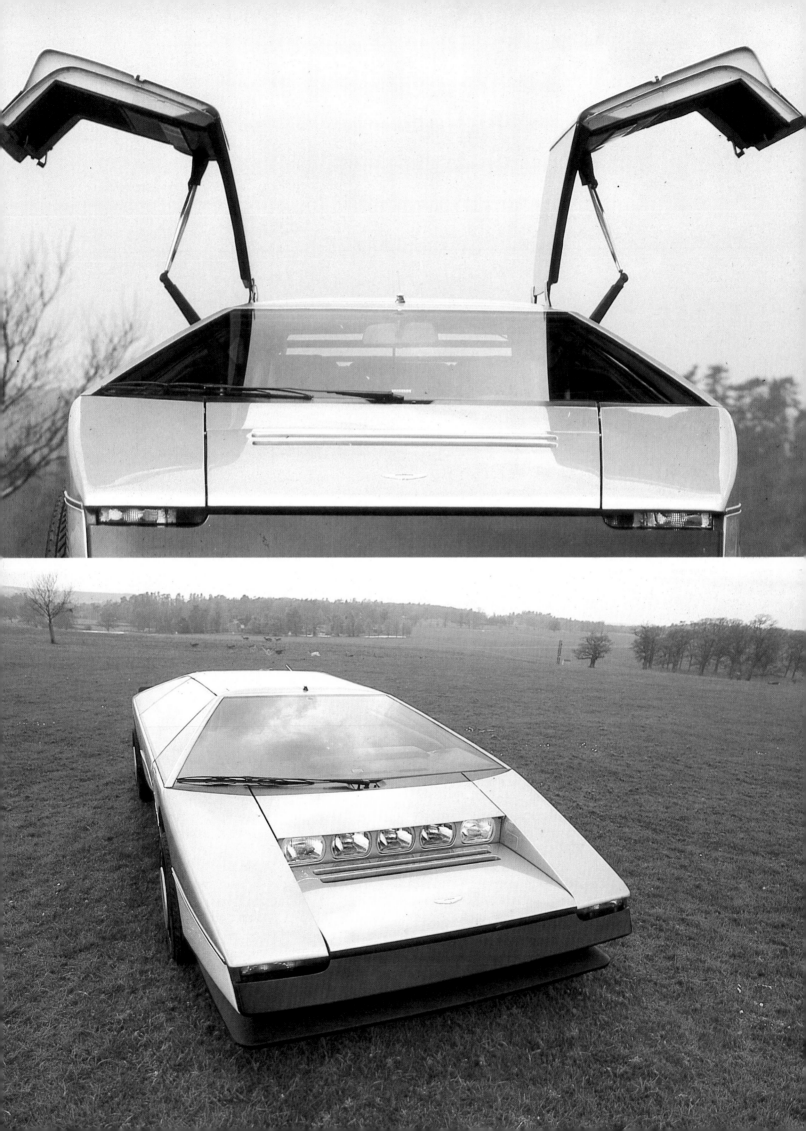

Lagonda runs very smoothly too. The long flat bonnet conceals the tried and tested Aston Martin V-8 engine; the pistons move in sequence at 90°. At 5,500 rpm, the Lagonda gets 320 hp together : Enough to take 5 people and their luggage from 0 to 60 mph in about 7 seconds and to convey them at 140 mph on freeways. The happy few who have had a chance to test drive the Lagonda, find it also extremely comfortable. The engine noise is confined to a background hum, the suspension is said to be very agreeable and so are the seats, upholstered in top quality Conolly leather (like Rolls-Royces). Efficient air-conditioning means the driver always keeps a cool head. The single-spoke steering-wheel is 14″ across. Power steering is reduced as speed increases. Indeed, 125 mph is no speed to lose your grip at.

However, one customer who visited the Aston Martin factory in 1979 did seem to lose his grip on reality. He came, of course, from the Middle East where oil and dollars are gushing out, and he expressed a rather special wish. That young man found the Aston Martin Lagonda just boring. He wanted to be spared the humiliation of meeting the same car somewhere along the road. To avoid such cruel fate, he demanded exclusivity. He needed an absolutely unique car — A one-off model. As silent as the Lagonda, but with seagull doors and more power under the bonnet, naturally. Well, so be it!

The order was quite clear : "Build the fastest car in the world for me". To win the confidence of the Englishmen, he made a down payment, cash in hand: Some say it was 100,000 pounds.

Car stylist William Towns was immediately summonned. He was delighted to have a free hand and set to work straight away. His drawing-board gave birth to an extraordinary design: Extra-low (43 in.

high), extra-wide (61.4 in. wide) with flat surfaces everywhere, like the Lagonda. This, plus Pirelli's extra-wide racing tires made for a breathtaking effect.

But, right in the middle of the job, came a shattering piece of news: the Middle Eastern customer had changed his mind and cancelled the order. Because of his spendthrift ways, his family had had to clip his wings somewhat.

But the British are made of sterner stuff... and the Aston Martin team, far from being discouraged, made a quick decision: "Well, we'll build the "Bulldog" — for that was the name of the super-racing car — just for ourselves." Some plausible explanation had to be found for the Press. Easy enough: "With the "Bulldog", we want to show that we are also capable of building the ultimate in automobiles. We want to fly the flag of the British car industry and take our place as creative designers among other industrial groups."

In any case, the firm's achievement did not escape notice. The Bulldog was the star of the Los Angeles and Tokyo Shows because, apart from its spectacular styling, it has a host of interesting technical features. Thus, the Aston Martin V-8 engine has been souped up by two turbochargers by Garrett Air Research and has a raring 600 hp under the bonnet. Apart from that, the Bulldog has what it takes to leave others standing, however superlative they may be: Porsche Turbo, Ferrari Berlinetta Boxer, or Maserati Khamsin. Chief Engineer Keith Martin swears that the Bulldog will go up to 190 mph. Naturally, nobody has tested it yet, because nobody has found near the factory a straight stretch of road long enough to reach that speed.

HEULIEZ

From the Horses of Yesteryear to Computers

The Heuliez bodyshop started with the production of horsedrawn carriages in 1922. A half-century later it has become an industrial concern with ultramodern production facilities and design department.

Yves Dubernard, the head of design at Heuliez, looks on the future optimistically. Since 1979 the French firm has a brand new research and develop-

ment facility, built on a twelve-acre lot near the Cerizay factory in western France. "Next to the production facilities, this research center will be our second leg for the future," explains Dubernard. Here, as at General Motors and Volkswagen, the computer has already largely replaced the drawing board. Strength testing, new materials testing and aerodynamic research can now all be simulated on the CRT display. In fact, it comes as no surprise when major automakers, overloaded with work, subcontract their design projects to Heuliez. And Heuliez has generally proved capable of performing such work more quickly and at lower cost. Besides this, the Heuliez plant is backed by state-of-the-art facilities for prototype production. "We can do a job

Peugeot 604 limousine.

154

in six months that it takes the majors three years to accomplish," says Yves Dubernard. Indeed, Heuliez technicians and workers can have complete cars on wheels and ready to drive in record time. Many of the company's customers call on it to develop alternative versions of their own prototypes: fresh insights never hurt. It's also the reason why many clients elect to remain anonymous and why so many of the cars produced at Cerizay are never known to the public. Of course it's no secret that Renault and Citroën, as well as some leading foreign automakers, regularly subcontract to Heuliez. But the customer core also includes firms from Venezuela, Egypt and Zaire, as well as the French Army, the French Railways and airport authorities.

Heuliez's highly advanced production plant puts out not only passenger cars, but also trucks, buses and special-purpose vehicles. Moreover, Heuliez's broad experience in the area of plastics processing has further enhanced its reputation with leading automakers. Thus, Heuliez makes both the rally version of the Citroën Visa, called the Chrono, and the body of the Renault 5 Turbo.

Recently, Heuliez has sought to return to the market with its own product line. For example, there's the handsome Renault Fuego convertible whose top closes automatically at the touch of a button. Yves Dubernard accomplished this by first acquiring two old American convertibles from the '60s to study their roof mechanism, in view of the

Renault Fuego cabriolet ▶.

Talbot-Wind.

American automakers' unequalled experience in this field. The result — the Renault Fuego convertible — is not only a fine-looking, gutsy design, but also a good all around car.

Similarly, the body for the Citroën Chrono, built for rallying, presented quite a challenge to Duber-nard. Yet he soon "civilized" the small 90-hp car with a top speed of 110 mph providing it with perfectly matched colors of metallic paint and fine leather trim interior, to produce a real little jewel box. On the other hand, the Peugeot 604 "limo" is more suited to V.I.P.s and top executives. Derived from the 604, and generally from the 142 hp "STi" version, this limousine has seen its already considerable wheelbase extended by another 24 in., resulting in a real monster of a car, measuring 210 in. long. This has made it possible to add a row of jump seats at mid-body, or simply to stretch ones legs. The 604 "long-car" affords all the comforts of the great American limousines and a customer can order every possible luxury option he can dream of, including air conditioning, liquor cabinet, 140-watt stereo, speed control. It is truly an experience to glide silently at 95 mph down the highway, stretching your legs as far as they'll go.

Citroën Visa Chrono.

CITROËN

CITROËN PENTHOUSE CX

The Easy Life

When the design department of a major automaker decides to have some fun...

Just wave your hand about your wrist and whisper, "Oh là là" and you'll be doing what every Frenchman does when he sees a Penthouse CX coming his way. The Citroën engineers produced this unique work as a gag for the Paris Auto Show. Actually, Citroën's CX provides an ideal basis for this kind of whims. Its front-wheel drive and hydro-pneumatic suspension make it possible to add even large and heavy parts without becoming involved in major technical alterations. Since the CX is sometimes converted into an ambulance or a van, why not turn it into a mobile home? As a first step, the vehicle was given a second rear axle; then they really went to work on it. The huge body allows passengers to remain standing; when the bed is pulled down, two people can sleep in it — really sleep. Then there are all the little things that make life easy: radio-alarm clock, stereo sound system and color TV. There's also a radiator to warm the occupants, and, naturally, a coffee machine. The bathroom includes a toilet, a "bidet" and a sink. Insurance against water shortage is provided by a 200-liter tank at the rear of the machine. Finally, there's a generator set to power the electric lights and the refrigerator.

TONY RUSSEL

NANCY

A Modern French Ro 80

By borrowing the engine from the
NSU Ro 80 and parts of modern sports car
bodies, Frenchman Rony Russel has made a
highly personal dream NSU Ro 80.

"For me, the NSU Ro 80 is still a car ahead of its
time, even today" says Tony Russel from Reims.
Tony used to be a stunt-man and he quite knows
what he's talking about: for the last 15 years, he's
spent all his free time on his favorite hobby —
building cars. He built several cars derived from
Volkswagens and Renaults, then, in 1974, he went
on to his most ambitious project yet: "I wanted to
build a four-seater sports car, something like the
Lamborghini Marzal designed by Bertone. »

For the engine, the only possible answer was the
NSU Ro 80, since the very flat front could only
accommodate the very compact 2-rotor Wankel
engine. All the other engines were too bulky or
lacked power. However, Russel's taste for the Ro 80
did not stop at the engine — he also adopted the
transmission with front-wheel drive, chassis and
suspension! Of course, this choice made things easier
for him too, because he could not afford to fully
redesign the car. Money was always a problem: "I
never thought this project would cost me about
400 000 French francs."

The outcome, after 8 years, is a resounding
success: A plastic-bodied 4-door, 5-seater sports car.
As low-slung as a Ferrari, with front fold-doors like
the Lamborghini Countach and rear gullwing doors,
like the Mercedes 300 SL.

Naturally, Tony Russel has not yet had any buyer
interested in the "Nancy", although he would be
delighted to fill the financial gap. However, as
parting is always painful, he would like to be
properly compensated for such a loss. For the
moment, his offspring is in a Museum. Which one?
The Nancy Automobile Museum, of course!

WOLFRACE

A Six-Wheel Spaceship

British wheel maker Wolfrace devotes considerable attention to his image. After making a first sensation with a six-wheeled Range Rover, he produced an even more dramatic car — the six-wheeled, two-engined "Sonic".

Looking at this car, one gets the feeling that it has come straight out of a science fiction movie. In fact, the car has very little in common with a normal car. At the front, four leading wheels determine steering. The two side-by-side engines drive one rear wheel each, via automatic transmissions, with a computer controlling their synchronization. Eight V-mounted cylinders provide a 3.5 liter displacement, giving each engine a power of 250 hp. Wolfrace claims a drag coefficient for the Sonic's ultra-flat fiberglass body even below the ideal 0.30 threshold, providing

Wolfrace Sonic.

top speed expectations of as high as 185 mph. And the analogies with aeronautic construction don't stop there: each of the two cockpits is fully instrumented and even the passenger can check revs or oil temperature. Instead of the usual pointers, the instruments feature digital LCD display technology. True to England's tradition of tolerance, the "Sonic" has been approved for road traffic.

Nodoby was really much surprised when Wolfrace, the well-known, light-alloy rim manufacturer decided that the Range Rover was lacking wheels... However, the Range initially designed as an advertising gag with an extra rear axle, not only provided evidence of its improved drive capacity in cross-country driving, but also of increased loading capacity and roominess.

The "climber" soon found its feet as a fire-truck in airfields and as a rescue vehicle.

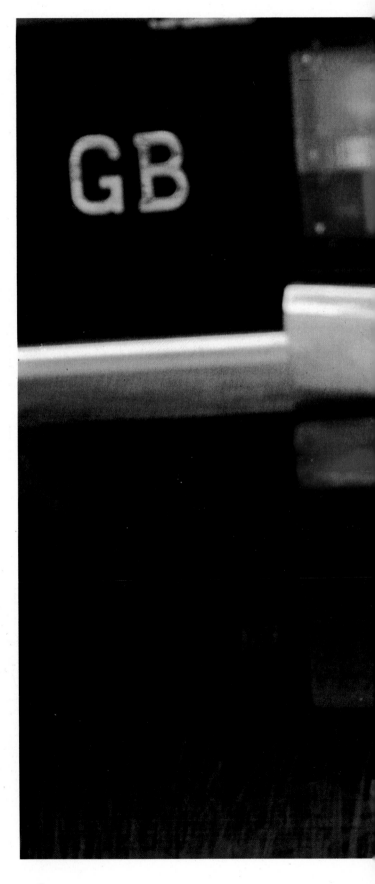

Wolfrace Range 6

Matra Rancho.

a spade and a fisherman's net. These, together with a diving mask, underscore the special penchant of this man from the Basque country for nautical sports. The modified Rancho is further provided with wooden bumpers. A leisure vehicle? That's what he seems to have intended, especially when you consider that he next turned his attention to a Mercedes G. Care to guess the color?

PIERRE CARDIN

SBARRO STASH

Pierre Cardin, the Parisian couture designer himself deemed the Stash worthy of an incursion into the realm of the automobile. This man of many talents, who has dressed up models, and chocolate and coffee-machines as well; who has designed furniture, has built a dining empire around Maxim's and restyled a jet plane with the stroke of his pencil showed elegant restraint when it came to car design. The fiberglass coupe in question has been given noble fabrics, a painted, laminated rubber facia, and color-matched striped seats and carpets. Technically, Cardin has been almost conservative : the car is powered by a rear, Volkswagen K 70 engine — a rather shy powerplant for Sbarro's ambitions, but yielding a price of 65,000 Swiss francs. As Franco Sbarro himself puts it: "The Stash is good looking, very convenient and relatively inexpensive." In spite of this, only a small number — five in fact — have been built to date. As usual with Sbarro, customers may choose the engine. If the K 70 seems a bit rickety, you can order a Stash with a 6.9-liter Mercedes 450 SE engine. The Stuttgart eighter, needless to say, will turn your Stash into a custom bombshell topping 155 mph.

WALTER WOLF

WOLF LAMBORGHINI LP 500

There's nothing surprising about a Formula One team boss treating himself to an exotic car. Except that he could never buy the engine of this Lamborghini!

Walter Wolf is no fashion designer, but a businessman. His automotive prestige is due neither to fancifulness nor to his mechanical expertise, but rather entirely to his outstanding performance as

sponsor and manager of the Formula One team that bears his name. Specifically, for those who made it to the pits of a Grand Prix track some time between 1975 and 1980, Wolf is the name that appeared on a four-wheeled monster — the Lamborghini specially made to his order.

The first Wolf Lamborghini LP 500 S, produced in 1975, was red, with black wings and an adjustable tail fin. Hardly a car to go unnoticed! The second version however was immediately toned

down. It was royal blue with gold fillets and the "Maple Leaf" emblem emphasizing Wolf's Canadian origins.

One crucial detail of the latter design is that the tail fin is electrically controlled from the driver's seat like a rearview mirror. At 185 mph, that's enough to convert the Wolf car into a Wolf airplane perhaps more effective on take-off than safe on landing. This second Wolf was certainly the most fascinating Lamborghini ever built — even more successfully styled than the third. As for the 5-liter engine, our wealthy top executive of Wolf Racing somehow never managed to buy it. It was a one-of-a-kind engine to which the factory never gave up title, allowing it out for each new car... on loan! In fact the production Lamborghinis come with a 4-liter engine. The 5-liter Wolf special was transferred from car to car as the bodies changed, and each time Wolf resold a Lamborghini, a "standard" 4-liter went with it.

The most dazzling women lounge nonchalantly in vast convertibles and the drivers jump out at every stop to buff-up the paintwork. There's a highly talented customizer concealed within every one of these car fiends. It is thus no surprise that the professionals of Puncto Finish are so much better than many of their European counterparts. For, as the saying goes in California: "Tell me what you drive, and I'll tell you who you are." This is why humorists refer to Los Angeles as "the world's greatest combustion engine".

AUBURN SPEEDSTER

Not Just the Replica of a Legend

They say that Marlene Dietrich, on first seeing a white 1935-vintage Auburn Speedster, cried out: "It's a cloud!" Reason enough to accept the fact that the Auburn was considered one of the most beautiful sports cars of its time. Besides, the Auburn displayed its goods as openly as beautiful Marlene. Remember Marlene's unabashed display of leg as Lola the coquette in "The Blue Angel".

Well, the Auburn too liked to show her bod. She *had* to. Because in 1935, she was the great white hope, expected to turn around the slumping sales of the Auburn company. The car was the brainchild of engineer August Duesenberg and body builder Gordon Miller Buehrig who designed the eternal marvel and sold it for the comparatively low price of $2,245. As it were though, they sold only 600. Was it too cheap? That's a possibility, since the high society people in those days wouldn't even look at a car that carried a less-than-five-figure price tag. Marlene though, didn't need that kind of magnet, getting all the attention she wanted with no car at all. So she bought a Speedster and by the same token became the most famous Auburn driver ever. New competition may be on its way though, as this beautiful car has been in production again for a couple of years in Pasadena. Evidently, "California Custom Coach Incorporated" means to right the wrong treatment given to the two-seater. On the outside, California Custom's replica is an exact copy of the original. But under the fiberglass hood, things start to happen. The new Auburn has a modern Ford V8 engine and automatic transmission and tops at 125 mph compared to 105 for the old Speedster.

CLENET

A Frenchman in America

A 39-year-old Frenchman, Alain Jean-Marie Clenet, a graduate of École Supérieure de Design Industriel de Paris, has made his dream-car reality in Santa Barbara, California.

Clenet, with this "Clenet Continental", has connected up with the tradition of the legendary sports cars of the thirties. This car's huge hood, its shortened rear end, curving fenders and chrome side exhausts really to remind one of the Golden Age of automaking. Clenet maintains that he hasn't produced a replica, but rather a "very special car" for a "very special era". Once inside, the passengers find themselves surrounded by the finest leather, sheepskin and exotic wood. Beneath the hood, things are a little less refined, but still "comfortable". There's a 5.7-liter Ford V8 engine working in near-perfect silence and the automatic transmission is smooth. This car weighs 4080 lbs and is 222.4 in. long, which is quite impressive, even by American standards.

As charming and elegant as a young French lover willing to make a conquest of Hollywood studios, 39-year-old Clenet loves to define his work simply — may be a bit too simply: "My intention is to build the best possible automobiles, but in very small numbers so that they be truly individualized. I think that's all what I do. » It should be added that this son of a motor tradesman and a former Tour de France racing driver has long been help up as an

194

example for French success in the United States. At the age of 21, in 1965, he set out for Detroit with his French engineer's and designer's diplomas; in 1975, he founded his own business — Clenet Coachworks, Inc. — in Santa Barbara, California. The small workshop has gradually turned into a real luxury car business, since 250 units from his initial roadster series were soon ordered by American V.I.P.s. From the very beginning, the Clenet has been recognized as *the* car. You could see jet setters, businessmen and movie stars at the wheel of a Clenet, wearing Ray Ban sunglasses and nonchalantly leaving their cigars in the crystal ashtray, while driving on Beverley Hills' Rodeo Drive or to Westhampton's most distinctive golf courses.

Today, the $70,000-worth Clenet is still a great classic to automobile connoisseurs. Having to cope with expansion problems, Clenet was forced to enlarge his workshops and there were fears that his financial balance might be in jeopardy. But this did not prevent him from producing two further, splendid achievements: the Series II convertible and the brand new, integral-body Asha. Clenet's production plans aim at 500 units, at a unit price of $78,500, which leads Alain Jean-Marie (Clenet) to say: "I sincerely believe that Clenets do embody a combination of modern U.S. technology and European craftsmanship. By their very nature, Clenets are unique luxury cars... In this way, I think I've been successful. »

STUTZ

The Revival of a Great Classic

At the turn of the twenties, Stutz was a name best known in America. And this is the tradition which the builder of today's Stutz — the "Blackhawk" — wanted to stick to.

The Blackhawk's designers weren't at all interested in replicating an antique model in terms of styling. Instead, they set out to achieve the much more difficult task of integrating prewar body parts into a modern design. Did they succed? We'll leave that up to the beholder. In any case, the initial idea has been materialized: curving fenders, a classic radiator grille, the spare wheel mounted on the trunk and external exhaust pipes give the Blackhawk that certain look that eliminates any doubts. Moreover, the body and its assembly were not carried out in the U.S.; rather, they were crafted by expert Italian hands in the Modena "Carozzeria Padana" bodyshop. That's also where the Blackhawk's General Motors powerplant is fitted.

The V8 engine can be had with 5 to 8·2 liters displacement, to suit the customer. Its most powerful version generates 400 Hp, giving the Stutz a top speed of 125 mph. Don't expect any more, for the car's aerodynamics are rather unpretentious...

Now, some information for technical detail lovers. The car is 226·7 in. long, 78·7 in. wide, and weighs 5 290-5 510 lbs., depending on its fittings. It is 54 in. high, and has a "small" 25-gallon fuel tank. To speak of fuel consumption or price would be bad taste; however, to those who hesitate, Stutz offers a whole range of bodies (and colors) for the 4-door "Bearcat" convertible, a car which, in the builder's opinion, offers its passengers the room and luxury they deserve — a two-edged formula, since

Stutz Blackhawk

the Diplomatic sedan, extended by 27·5 in., additionally offers flap seats (room-wise) and a TV set (luxury-wise).

Nevertheless, for Harry C. Stutz who founded the marque in Indianapolis in 1913, those odd figures produced seventy years later should be regarded as a tribute to his cars, of which the most celebrated was no doubt the Stutz Canonball that has beaten in 1916 the U.S. "Coast-to-Coast" record. So, those incredibly luxurious Stutz cars which had disappeared after the great depression, have been revived since 1971 thanks to a Chrysler stylist, Virgil M. Exner, and a banker, James O'Donnell. This was

the least that could be done, since in theory there is nothing too beautiful or too expensive for a Stutz. Gold is often used for switches, handles or interior screws.

However, within this often baffling range, the palm is borne by the royal limousine built for King Khalid on the basis of a Blackhawk. Among other fittings, there is a swivelling throne that can be lifted for the King to appear through the sliding roof. The car is 296 in. long and weighs 3 tons.

For whom this type of vehicle may be of interest, we shall remind that Stutz's corporate office is in New York, on Fifth Avenue naturally.

Stutz Blackhawk.

200

AMERICAN CUSTOM COACHWORKS (ACC)

The Beverly Hills Designer

Based in Los Angeles' most select neighborhood, car designer ACC has specialized in serving movie stars and the aristocracy of money gravitating around them. It has a penchant for Cadillacs.

"We build our cars in the image of America", asserts the American Coachworks team, meaning on a solid basis. The decline of the Detroit dinosaurs has opened up a highly profitable market for body builders, for in Beverly Hills, at least since the advent of Ronald Reagan, the demand for Great American Masterpieces has grown dramatically. Thus is a Fleetwood Cadillac sawed in half and extended by a full meter to add a row of seats or merely to provide more leg room. A glass partition ensures privacy from the chauffeur, while privacy vis-à-vis the exterior is provided by black-tinted rear and side windows. All comfort features have been moved to

the back: air conditioning, stereo sound system and bar. The remainder of accommodations for this living room are custom-built for each individual customer, who can ask for woodwork of aged German oak or English walnut, for crystal lighting fixtures or for a fully equipped secretarial corner. About 14 weeks are required for delivery and the starting price is 60,000 dollars — an investment made by some 800 customers since the establishment of ACC.

So, ACC's business is highly successful — which seems « normal » at a time when it is not possible to get access to a fashionable night spot in the United States if the doorman hasn't seen you getting out of a limousine at least as long as the shortest one produced by ACC. No question in 1983 to appear at a Hollywood preview evening or to hope being admitted to Régine's New York club if you've used an ordinary yellow cab. Nowadays, the big limousine has become a must. ACC managed to steadily produce that type of cars when competitors, such as Bradley in Florida, were forced to shift to the production of small electric-motor cars. However, nobody in the U.S. can trust to be definitely

Cadillac Fleetwood.

successful in the field of dream cars, as new entrepreneurs are always ready to tackle that type of market with increasingly astounding vehicles. Maybe that's why ACC have added strings to their bow.

For more sporty personalities, American Coachworks has opened up a second, equally successful, department which builds coupes and convertibles, again preferably based on Cadillacs. This is usually done by completely reworking the proportions of large limousines, the motto being: "more in the front, less in the rear". The front doors begin where the rear doors used to end. If a customer finds this two-seater too short, ACC will add another meter of sheet metal between the door frame and the wheel well. On request, spare wheels may be attached in this space, as on prewar cars. Naturally, the wheel disks are provided with dummy spokes. The American predilection for baroque styling is indulged wherever possible, just as in those Disneylandish imitations of the Chateau de Versailles sometimes found among the superb mansions of Beverly Hills.

MARDIKIAN

American Trim for European Supercars

Albert Mardikian, based in Newport Beach, near Los Angeles, specializies in customizing "European beauties". No doubt, as an importer of BMWs, Porsches, Mercedes, Citroëns, Rolls-Royces, Ferraris and Lamborghinis, he hardly lacks top-quality raw materials. As the first thing that must be done to these beauties is to adjust them to the stringent U.S. safety emissions control regulations. Mardikian has also specialized in "federalizing" foreign cars for U.S. approval. Next, he puts his stamp on them. For instance, he added a dual turbocharger to the Ferrari Boxer and the Lamborghini Countach... in a country where the highest speed limit is 55 mph! And for the BMW M1, he has set up his own, limited production series.

The well-known American trade magazine "Road and Track" has given high praise to one of the customized Ferraris, stating that, "The Commendatore himself would be proud to pose next to this car. The detailing is even better than the outstanding trim of the original Ferrari".

Surely enough, this Broxer — renamed Mardikian 512 BBS Turbo — has great style, and the 700 hp announced by the firm give you the shivers.

It takes Mardikian a year to build this Ferrari 400 he extends by 75 in., hand-made of course. The only effort required from the buyer is to sign a check. A $250,000 check, though.

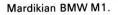

Mardikian BMW M1.

Mardikian Ferrari 400.

On the other hand, the Mardikian 350 GTS must give the Commendatore the shivers to see it. Actually, it is a rather true replica of the 365 GTS 4 Daytona, but for a few details: it is a convertible powered by a two-turbocharger, Chevrolet Corvette engine! According to the car's data sheet, this powerplant helps it generate 500 hp and reach a top speed of 198 mph.

An importer and a customizer, Albert Mardikian has now taken on a new dimension: He "exports" his Californian cars to his Texas dearlerships and plans to establish a further shop in Florida. As can be seen from the pictures here, the Mardikians have a highly personal look. The BMW M1, with its 300 hp, its sliding roof and its air-conditioning system (from General Motors, naturally), however means for the buyer a capital investment of $115,000... And, as we've seen, it is not Mardikian's most sophisticated car.

VECTOR

Hedgehopping with the Latest Space
Technology

Americans have a taste for superlatives. The
makers of the Vector are no exception: they
describe their car as "the world's fastest
production car" and as the first American car
"better than the best European sports cars".

Everyone has heard of the "Strand" in Venice,
California, that hangout for fringe groups and freaks
of all kinds. One handful of creative car freaks —
Vector Cars — has set up shop within reach of the
Strand to build a virtual road-jet. According to its
designer, Gerald Wiegert, "The Vector sets new
criteria by which all other sports cars will be judged
from hereon". In fact, adds Wiegert, "The Vector
has nothing in common with other exotic cars. We
didn't intend to remake Porsche, Ferrari or Lamborghini. What we wanted was to build the most

advanced sports car in the world". In view of this goal, Wiegert drew upon the latest space technology available whenever possible, starting with the engine. He added two turbochargers to boost the output of an already outstanding Chevrolet V8 engine. As a result, he claims 640 hp for the power machine, which is fitted with the same three-speed automatic transmission traditionally used on most American dragsters. The Vector reaches 100 mph in first gear and 112 mph in second gear. It's top speed should be about 230 mph, which would make it as fast as the racing cars that come out on top at the Le Mans 24-hour event. The frame, like that of a modern jet fighter, is a single-shell aluminum and plastic construction; the body is made of high-strength, ultra-light Kevlar. The front and rear are of flexible plastic, deformable protective elements which will absorb any impact energy. The transversally-mounted engine is attached with just a small number of bolts which have been made easily accessible to enable easy engine removal. The interior space also looks a lot like a fighter cockpit, particularly since some of the dashboard instruments come straight from aeronautics, along with the 5-point safety belts. This low-flying plane sells for roughly 150,000 dollars.